4/12

Rain

Rain

Winner of the 2005 Verse Prize

Jon Woodward

Hi Amanda,
Nice to meet you! Have a
good day.

WAVE BOOKS

SEATTLE / NEW YORK

Published by Wave Books
www.wavepoetry.com

Wave Books titles are distributed to the trade by
Consortium Book Sales and Distribution
1045 Westgate Drive, St. Paul, Minnesota 55114

Library of Congress Cataloging-in-Publication Data:

Woodward, Jon, 1978-
  Rain / Jon Woodward.— 1st ed.
    p. cm.
  "Winner of the 2005 Verse Prize."
  ISBN 1-933517-14-X (trade pbk. : alk. paper) — ISBN 1-933517-15-8
(alk. paper)
  I. Title.

PS3623.O685R35 2006
811'.6—dc22

2006000038

Designed and composed by Mark Abrams
Printed in the United States of America

9 8 7 6 5 4 3 2 1

FIRST EDITION

Wave Books 007

Contents

Spring (Comprising Further Music)

[in spite of which it's] 3
[it's going to rain I'm] 4
[the man who sells me] 5
[completely naïve oriole earlier the] 6
[the old man down the] 7
[and so the strawberry sitting] 8

Rain, Ocean

[Patrick and I sat at] 11
[a grown man the singer] 12
[the anecdote that a man] 13
[each egg had only one] 14
[he said writing the novel's] 15
[it's not that he died] 16
[don't know why he keeps] 17
[it's okay when a mammal] 18
[all the stopping and starting] 19
[a man in a gray] 20
[here in 1625 Gov Roger] 21
[I had feared it I] 22
[the water was where my] 23
[although I didn't once fear] 24

Attempt

[but the house sparrows are] 27
[don't get me wrong there] 28
[this weather's the actual God] 29
[some church I guess down] 30
[in a terrible] 31
[I have to think up] 32

The Long Night of Ezekiel

[the tar they use to] 35
[newer sore spots blossomed open] 36
[the stairs will require explanation] 37
[down the world's largest hand] 38
[your eyes are just hanging] 39
[I know enough I resist] 40
[in the book of Ezekiel] 41
[climbing I radioed my father] 42
[some fire extinguishers are obviously] 43
[tulips start to look all] 44
[today has been a particularly] 45
[only half of the house] 46
[looking over the bomb inventory] 47
[only half of the house] 48
[the bomber swept lower and] 49
[for weeks toward the end] 50
[only half of the house] 51
[is that all you do] 52
[oh little skins oh warm] 53

[locked out in the rain] 54

[whatever it was that tripped] 55

Leap

[it was a spider dangling] 59

[this is the second shower] 60

[I had no business blowing] 61

[a maniac is what drives] 62

[the eye a plastic bubble] 63

[are we to understand that] 64

Love Poems and Myopia

[telling Oni how I was] 67

[it seemed so easy and] 68

[what a myopia needs is] 69

[surprise John Donne wants me] 70

[sleep is a brick floor] 71

[spring became late summer early] 72

[we're going to need someplace] 73

[they're putting these hubcaps on] 74

Spring (Comprising Further Music)

in spite of which it's
hard to imagine it all
going to shit the pinkflowering
dogwood for example is my
newest favorite tree the decay

of what world we've got's
not exactly what I'm afraid
of not now the woman
brings the cheeseburger I ordered
here come the selections the

jukebox converted five of my
quarters into in the correct
order what questions then to
ask for what if anything
about this coffee these fries

it's going to rain I'm
going to go see Spider
Man by the time the
theater lets out it'll be
raining I won't have seen

it start I'll have been
watching a boy turn into
a spider I saw something
on TV last night a
sort of round window admitting

golden light into a room
where a young man sat
staring out the window at
a head high pile of
what looked like scrap metal

the man who sells me
fruit from his stand is
either a very pensive man
or a little slow just
now on the sidewalk I

found a tiny egg cracked
open on one side its
shell is speckled like oatmeal
I'll have to look up
what bird might have laid

it inside there's a moist
pink indistinctness with a black
spot I assume was becoming
the eye also there's a
little yolk left not much

completely naïve oriole earlier the
orange opposite of camouflage analogous
to the little ditty he
and I exchanged whistling back
and forth I got him

to follow me five blocks
before he figured me out
the kingfisher was the other
story warcrying like a ratchet
for only impossible reasons then

dropping into his pond reemerging
with a goldfish flapping out
the side of his mouth
slapping it against a branch
to arrive at an understanding

the old man down the
hall the one that's always
coughing recently returned from China
I'd thought he was dead
I worry he can hear

me masturbating at night I
try to keep quiet or
to mask my sound flip
on the radio Eleanor Rigby
picks up the rice and

so forth she never outlives
her own song nobody once
pauses to think blinking breathing
standing naked eviscerated ah look
at all the lonely etcetera

and so the strawberry sitting
alone on a small table
as its seeds arranged in
a Fibonacci spiral network begin
to split and unlid themselves

eyes each winking open brings
a world into focus funnels
it in through each tiny
opening keeping it trapped there
listen do you hear the

eyes crying out no they
can't cry out of course
not the silence is pure
now pick up the strawberry
put it in your mouth

Rain, Ocean

Patrick and I sat at
the bus stop he was
only going to be in
town for a day we
were talking about how some

things look like other things
it's one of the seven
basic conversations then he said
a thing here reproduced what
a brutally fascinating world it

was stirring if a little
extrapolatory he could only have
been able to see a
tiny part of the world
from where we were sitting

a grown man the singer
in Patrick's band is singing
songs he wrote about the
sun the band's the reason
why Patrick came to town

he explains how this man
deliberately attempted to wall off
all of his anxieties by
singing about the sunshine it
couldn't possibly work I tried

dancing at their show a
first for me but can't
help overhearing the death stumbling
fear look at all these
idiots dancing I'm fucking surrounded

the anecdote that a man
in a world sneezed and
waited and waited for someone
nearby to bless him or
at least to say bless

you and the resultant limbo
my friend's novel has he
says the tension between disorientation
and clarity at its center
and so will tomorrow morning's

scrambled eggs he talks about
these lighted antenna towers outside
our college town I know
nothing about them other than
that he's talking about them

each egg had only one
parent likely not the same
as the others and since
these three eggs are scrambled
they probably had three parents

is that an unusual heritage
for a breakfast to have
also for breakfast I'm having
a headache somebody was serving
the poorest ever stab at

sangria I stood blabbing in
the rain with girls and
sang Beatles tunes banged on
pans with wooden spoons nobody
wasn't singing nor was listening

he said writing the novel's
just an excuse for us
to discuss it interrupted himself
this scotch tastes he said
like a goddamn kickball and

then had to leave and
he grabbèd my wrist by
way of goodbye and said
Jesus Jon I fuckin' loveya
I grabbed the wrist of

the arm grabbing mine and
it was the trapeze for
a second y'know fear Patrick
says terror's funny but at
the moment I'm hard pressed

it's not that he died
it's that he won't stop
dying and reemerging fully ordinarily
through ordinary doors saying in
his own voice hey brother

if he were in fact
my brother one says the
air keeps getting warmer being
that it's spring the trees
are all telling the same

story hone it down plunge
it with the piano music
we just listened to into
a bottle it won't help
him untwist from his rope

don't know why he keeps
dying these two girls kept
giving us shit then flitted
like packs of playing cards
sprayed made a mess of

the house and of the
party Patrick stood in a bucket
and died only one foot
could fit in the bucket
his whole body died as

he stood there would not
the body of Patrick this
bucket fit inside as the
bottle of my mouth fills
one of my head's pockets

it's okay when a mammal
breathes regularly my friend Patrick
came up from the drain
breathing like Stanley the Steam
Shovel I said hey you

wanna go to Gloucester and
look at how the tombstones
and fishing boat masts are
raised irregularly against the sky
he said nope I don't

isn't it observable that I'm
asleep let's go later meanwhile
mixed breaths like salad every
few intakes his sleep befuddles
itself hiccups and goes huh

all the stopping and starting
wears out the parts I
point out to Patrick a
metal beam holding part of
Gloucester up and rusting and

he withers I walk back
to the car and he's
already there another time I
was already at the car
when he walked back another

time I'm the only thing
on fire in a room
or the only thing not
in the room the book
he's reading snapping closed open

a man in a gray
T shirt is under a
boat the boat is not
in the water he's sitting
like a little boy and

turning a propeller on the
boat it's too rusty to
really want to turn anymore
a noise is produced I
think people are frowning at

Patrick and me because we
are ourselves frowning although not
because we're unhappy not five
minutes ago we were saying
how happy we are today

here in 1625 Gov Roger
Conant averted bloodshed between contending
factions one led by Myles
Standish of Plymouth the other
by Capt Hewes a notable

exemplification of arbitration in the
beginnings of New England two
black dogs are staring at
me and Patrick is dead
again and these dandelions which

obviously just came up are
dead too what we were
looking for was a big
rock into which a tale
of realized bloodshed had been

carved something along the lines
of here on this spot
in 1625 contending factions carved
each other's throats out you
can still see the stain

I had feared it I
was sitting in one crack
in the sidewalk when I
heard him ask me a
question from the most adjacent

crack he asked how is
your chowder we were both
eating chowder I was finding
mine uncomfortable but had gotten
used to it and managed

to convey that somehow then
we stood and walked not
exactly toward the ocean but
I would say that that
was where we ended up

the water was where my
headache was before it was
passed on to me the
water was a recording of
a voice saying you're welcome

by that time he'd spat
his cigarette out and lit
another and spat that one
out after smoking it this
is Patrick I'm talking about

the water went about sicking
up the water had climbed
down stairs the water purchased
me a seagull I'm a
trained seal I can't laugh

although I didn't once fear
being pushed into the water
as I almost always do
when standing next to a
body of water with almost

any other person

                        some
guy at a gas station

walked up to the car
began cleaning the windshield saying
as he did so Sic
Transit Gloria Patrick goes Sic
Transit my Chowder Shitting Ass

Attempt

but the house sparrows are
mating again each on top
of the other or sideways
flapping and chirping they're so
immodest so indiscriminate with each

other although it doesn't look
like it actually feels good
it looks like some voltage
is making them do it
but they do it regardless

and you don't see them
screaming in pain unless that's
what all that chirping is
we meanwhile couldn't have asked
for all our free will

don't get me wrong there
are some things about you
I find perfectly obnoxious that
I wouldn't want to change
look it's raining again we

needed another skin O come
be slender and true inside
the cemetery with me and
float up the hill towards
the tower O slide along

the aisles in the supermarket
with me see the organic
form the cans stacked on
more cans O the ribs
of the everyday metallic behemoth

this weather's the actual God
or at least it's that
honest moment before the concert
when the orchestra tunes itself
although much longer in duration

the instruments join in and
fall away as many times
as time will allow for
the droplets arrive at the
faces of you and me

and take with them as
they fall from our chins
the disinclination we or at
least I grew up with
nothing could compare to getting

rained on together the slick
of rainwater converts each thing's
outside to an image of
inside the only object without
a soul is the sun

some church I guess down
the street is tolling a
D flat over and over
twenty minutes now I wish
I'd been counting it'll probably

add up to thirty three
it's that time of year
this wonderful girl I met
last night either will or
will not end up all

tangled with lousy me with
my lousy arm hanging off
the side of the bed
with a pen hey wait
I think the bell stopped

in a terrible

accident I hope you're not
in a coma at the
hospital hope you just blew
me off guess I'm going
back to sleep but if

but if that isn't the
phone ringing hello oh Donald
Sutherland I was just watching
one of your movies what
say that again she's okay

oh Donald that's good news
hey you're a terrific actor
you could play a mean
God oh really I didn't
know that

I have to think up
things to say ahead of
time to keep from stuttering
when I speak it's the
only thing that works I've

got a brain full of
index cards you'd be appalled
unfortunately what I memorize is
obsolete almost immediately the conversation
veers unforeseeably and by the

time I got on the
bus it was raining and
it probably rained on you
as you walked home and
I'm sorry about that too

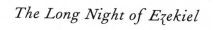

The Long Night of Ezekiel

the tar they use to
fill the cracks shines orange
from the orange streetlights but
is blacker than the asphalt
which doesn't shine nobody could've

made miles of something so
beautiful unintentionally but what's not
intentional the asphalt's made to
crack the tar and light
do their respective jobs deserted

playgrounds aren't more deserted on
nights when there's no wind
blowing and no less so
than the skeletons of half
buried nightmare animals they resemble

newer sore spots blossomed open
in the dam overnight full
wheelbarrows were brought we spent
all night and into the
morning trying to lick the

wounds closed my late grandmother
sat on top of the
dam it would've been unsafe
for a person but she'd
come back a sunlight finch

and vocalized for a while
by ten in the morning
the sun wasn't out yet
the dam gave way we
let it go what else

the stairs will require explanation
require rain cascading down them
you sit on a stair
rain sits down beside you
she finds out about you

explanation will require an extent
sitting on a stair your
body becomes a stair droplets
fall like bodies climbing down
the extent will require a

failure the clouds stack up
and lead me to the
tops of themselves or to
their middles the droplets fall
like stairs or bodies climbing

down they continue into the
ground the droplets keep falling
the stairs continue to descend
the street's a mere skin
what could be more permeable

down the world's largest hand
-dug well somewhere in Kansas
run unlit flights of stairs
individuals called tourists descend below
the daylight but not usually

very far but I made
it to the bottom the
prophet Ezekiel was there he
said he was building a
tiny ship inside a bottle

but it was too dark
to see then something licked
me in the darkness and
comprising further music Ezekiel turned
what black window on itself

your eyes are just hanging
there in their closets candy
coating would do them some
good hell candy coating would
be a real boon for

us all this morning when
I woke up I fabricated
the following nightmare you dangled
a microphone from your teeth
you were on a ledge

four stories up the microphone
swayed back and forth I
was jumping trying to grasp
it whaddaya mean not scary
I'll show you not scary

I know enough I resist
a padded room I dig
in my heels there is
nothing but the apocryphal to
find in straps and straitjackets

but something else is in
the heels of my shoes
that's why they took my
shoes away they left the
laces they tied them end

to end in a circle
held it up what's this
mean to you they asked
to me I asked yeah
you Trainwreck what's it mean

in the book of Ezekiel
a firetruck goes screaming down
Mass Ave and Ezekiel sees
the ladder it carries on
top of itself and writes

it's a beast that carries
its backbone on its back
and then he describes the
legs of the beast as
wheels that revolve but somehow

not within other wheels for
once and as you'd expect
if you know his style
he feels the heavy hand
of the Lord upon him

climbing I radioed my father
a peregrine falcon is up
here chasing to eat an
orange bird it looks like
a bright orange butterfly Dad

you have to get up
here see the way this
thing is dodging choosing wild
lines no number ever thought
of no equation the orange

bird is getting tired and
the falcon is sinking talons
into the flying flesh the
talons are disappearing Dad you've
got to get up here

some fire extinguishers are obviously
too small here's one the
size of my forearm I
can't imagine it putting anything
out it looks like you

could twist the top off
and there'd be hot soup
inside chicken noodle with vegetables
steam lightly rising off its
surface the phone rings hi

mom yeah I got it
it's right here thank you
no I like chicken noodle
the phone suddenly bursts into
flames um hold on mom

tulips start to look all
fucked up after they've been
open for awhile their petals
go lazy and strange it's
strange to see pictures of

my grandmother from when she
and grandpa got married they
weren't so bad looking they
didn't tell their friends where
they were honeymooning for fear

of practical jokes apparently these
same friends once turned all
the furniture in some house
upside down but given time
it might have happened anyway

today has been a particularly
but then otherwise it'd mean
have burned something to the
couldn't have stood it without
bridge or a building but

how could I help it
even my hilt is flammable
with the speed of a
printed circuit the prophet Ezekiel
spirited me from the zinnias

of fire what are you
get even a gasp of
at such a clip and
and for God's sake slow
the fuck go of my

only half of the house
was haunted in the non
-haunted half I found a
pantry with cans of corn
and pie filling and shelves

with honey and chocolate bars
and a fridge with leftover
macaroni casserole and chicken enchiladas
and a freezer with a
box of fudgesicles that were

made from all natural ingredients
on the box was a
picture of a penguin with
a red bowtie and a
top hat and a cane

looking over the bomb inventory
looking at the huge list
I heard the strangest music
my eyes were loudspeakers I
was shivering cold I must've

caught a bad fever the
local witch doctor stood my
ankles in a shallow place
in the river and affixed
good examples of a certain

kind of plant to me
in three places chest neck
and head I shivered I'm
made of molecules he said
over me certain preprogrammed words

only half of the house
was haunted in the non
-haunted half I found a
bra draped over a closet
door it was a pink

bra I guess it also
could've been black and lacy
or that color they call
nude there was a lamp
with a bright green shade

the switch for that lamp
was on the other side
of the room next to
the switch for the ceiling
fan which had four blades

the bomber swept lower and
lower in concentric circles we
felt bad about ourselves we
felt like dirt we had
poor self esteem the bomber

thanked us all for being
there but the way the
bomber said it made us
think he disagreed with himself
we added the bomber's name

to the list of people
we couldn't stand we also
were on that list and
at what point did the
bombs begin to fall exactly

for weeks toward the end
of the diary of Anne
Frank she and her family
ate nothing but strawberries they
canned them they made preserves

and jellies and ate as
many fresh as went into
the jars one of them
remarked that it looked as
if the whole world had

turned red meanwhile the war

suppose the authorities arrived and
led her family down the
stairs and out into the
sunshine what color what colors

only half of the house
was haunted at the boundary
between the two halves there
was a cold plaster wall
with a red door the

door was about eight feet
tall about four feet wide
maybe three inches thick but
that's just conjecture I don't
know how it sounded when

it was knocked on I
never knocked the red paint
was peeling off in several
places you could see all
the other colored layers underneath

is that all you do
is put things together I
asked the prophet Ezekiel what
he coughed do you mean
well I said when the

minotaur ate all those people
and coughed up their bones
you came along and put
them together again well Ezekiel
rebutted it was God who

did that and you my
friend you have made a
minotaur out of half a
bull and half a man
so just look who's talking

oh little skins oh warm
blooded from down the street
to us floats the sound
of the fleshhounds straining against
their window panes pressing their

incisors against the glass we
can't hear them saying their
small yet terrible things but
see the fog spreading like
a fog of semen on

the glass we are scatterfaced
feel full of gaps and
sure enough between these two
ribs is a gap big
enough for a canine tongue

locked out in the rain
on the fire escape begging
of the night shift lightning
god that one well aimed
bolt would cauterize the wound

left over where my ears
were pruned off please in
other words stop missing stop
yanking into clarity this galaxy
of droplets stop these snapshots

a whip of light lashes

my eyes and there's an
angel sitting next to me
on my bed a real
live angel he skips the
be ye not afraid stuff

son of man he says
may I try on a
pair of your running shoes
big surprise they don't fit

whatever it was that tripped
the latch we like actual
mammals run alongside it our
two eyes look in slightly
different directions neither is important

and our tongue is no
pointer either we are thirsty
we ducked in a shit
ditch an hour thought about
drinking it we ran on

and the thing that tripped
the latch ran on beside
us split a ripe cactus
with a glowing knife we
drank and rested and ran

Leap

it was a spider dangling
from my mail slot I
caught him in a drinking
glass Daring Jumping Spider *Phidippus*
audax I made him a

home in an empty salsa
jar he wasn't eating his
crickets I let him go
all of this strictly during
daylight hours it's good history

to claim it only happened
once but how then this
itching vestige looking closely enough
to see his retinas flash
who failed to free whom

this is the second shower
I've taken today I didn't
need to take this one
all I did today was
wake up and watch TV

at one point I walked
to the grocery store and
bought a pound of strawberries
for 99 cents they weren't
too tart if my body

is found I want them
to pack it with strawberries
I want my casket lined
with strawberries I want them
to bulldoze strawberries over me

I had no business blowing
mushroom clouds in the campfire
with 100 proof vodka I
could've killed myself it made
the girls there go oooooh

that always feels nice nobody
wants to start an argument
I could jump in front
of a car and I'd
probably survive they'd honk they'd

do anything to keep me
out of their car and
who'd blame them contrarily who
could fear death no more
spiked memories no foolish confrontations

just pure profit

a maniac is what drives
the bus I am alone
on the bus there are
twenty odd other people when
I was trying to count

just now we were at
a stop and some got
off and some got on
I lost track and not
going to start over the

maniac lobs syllables backwards at
us and jerks forward and
stops at stop lights I
wonder if all my currently
living grandparents are still alive

the eye a plastic bubble
filled with milk more than
twenty miles of visibility trapped
therein and it's a fine
day to jump out of

an airplane the doors open
and the suits full of
men leap from the gray
belly run and leap out
into and through fields of

temporary black flak marigolds blooming
and dissipating into air you're
always falling even inside the
plane into wide awakeness the
lights the wide aperture into

are we to understand that
the first man in front
of the bull and the
second man behind the bull
and the third in mid

leap are all the same
man that what is being
depicted is the leap itself
my eye at least agrees
with this triune depiction yesterday

today tomorrow which contains the
leap required to believe the
original leg leap yes can
get you up over the
charge of the outstretched bull

Love Poems and Myopia

telling Oni how I was
crying listening to a CD
of songs ostensibly about Anne
Frank that Patrick traded me
for a copy of Cat's

Cradle before he left and
she laughed not coldly but
more like she was saying
yeah I've felt silly crying
about perfectly deadly things too

we were walking along the
river under a sun so
bright that the voice of
the memory can't be heard
clearly and whether it speaks

out of or into the
past nobody's qualified to say
memory itself least of all
we sat down somewhere I
brought sandwiches she brought salad

it seemed so easy and
effortless we kissed and hugged
and wandered through some other
kind of night until the
blue day began to resume

again I remember seeing it
and commenting on it then
there was breakfast I took
a train and a bus
to get home nothing ever

fit me as comfortably as
those twenty four hours there
were little red mites climbing
the blue steps to my
place and purple irises opening

what a myopia needs is
to be subverted I've heard
people say love's subversive but
then I've heard people say
it's myopic there's this little

black cat Oni and I
meet sometimes when we go
out for a walk or
whatever he says meow at
us and runs over and

flops on his side we
pet him he rolls onto
his other side we pet
him some more he stands
up repeats the whole production

surprise John Donne wants me
not to be so dull
comma sublunary I badly misparaphrased
in my notebook a quote
from Villiers de L'Isle-Adam whoever

that is taken from a
Henry Corbin essay referring to
Messengers with Eyes of Clay
celestial angels my version reads
their irruption forms an aspect

of the credulity they inhabit
credulity versus ecstasy in the
original sea glass on the
beach every few steps she
picks up another similar piece

sleep is a brick floor
a vast and simple one
we breach out of it
and fall back in like
whales in the ocean I'll

be doing the dishes and
all of a sudden I'll
see my arm making nice
circle motions attached to my
wrist down inside a big

soapy pot where my hand
holds a scrubber thing and
digs it against the pot
moving by means of somehow
unknown and violent anticircular flexations

spring became late summer early
fall after midnight I got
up for some water her
apartment had grown cold a
chill wind gave lung motion

to the curtains words reasserting
themselves meaningless utterly meaningless the
eye never has enough of
seeing nor the ear its
fill of hearing this too

is meaningless a chasing after
the wind I stood still
next to the bed inside
the world as inside a
glacier creeping forward will it

grind us in its works
and if it does will
it matter as much as
it feels like it will
or is this also meaningless

we're going to need someplace
to go when we're done
here it doesn't need to
be heaven but I'll need
you there with me and

I'll need us to be
running all the trees and
rooms we've known will slip
past us and when they're
gone they'll be gone I

don't want to wake you
moving our arms around or
mumbling half words into the
dark but our situation by
virtue of being a situation

they're putting these hubcaps on
cars now which continue to
spin when the car comes
to a stop sleep is
a brick floor that goes

on forever we breach out
of it like whales out
of the ocean whales silhouetted
like souls what vast tracts
of muscle they must have

and from what depths they
must begin to gain enough
momentum to clear the water
and how they hang for
some seconds in the sun